waterfalls
and fountains

waterfalls and fountains

Philip Swindells

All inquiries should be addressed to:
Barron's Educational Series, Inc.
250 Wireless Boulevard
Hauppauge, New York 11788
http://www.barronseduc.com

International Standard Book Number 0-7641-1847-1
Library of Congress Catalog Card Number 2001091845

Printed in China
9 8 7 6 5 4 3 2 1

THE AUTHOR
Philip Swindells is a water gardening specialist with a long
experience of growing aquatic plants in many parts of the
world. In the U.K. he trained at the University of Cambridge
Botanic Garden and the famous aquatic nursery of Perrys of
Enfield, and ultimately became Curator of Harlow Carr
Botanical Gardens, Harrogate. The author of many
publications on water gardening, Philip was also formerly
the editor of the *Water Garden Journal* of the International
Waterlily Society, which in 1994 inducted him into their Hall
of Fame. He was awarded a Mary Hellier Scholarship in
1990 by the International Plant Propagator's Society for
pioneering work on the propagation of water lilies.

Acknowledgments
The publishers would like to thank the following
people for their valuable help and advice during the
preparation of this book: Anthony Archer-Wills,
Gail Paterson, and Emma Spicer at New Barn
Aquatic Nurseries, West Chiltington; Gill Page at
Murrells Nursery, Pulborough; Graham Quick for his
help with construction of the waterfalls; "G" and
colleagues at Old Barn Nurseries, Horsham; Graham
and Howard Healey at Four Seasons Bonsai Nursery,
East Peckham; and Stuart Thraves at Blagdon's,
Bridgwater.

contents

introduction

There is something about moving water that fascinates us. Regardless of our ages, water in all its gentle or turbulent moods holds most of us spellbound, be it the trickle of water over a stony streambed, the gentle flow from a fountain, or the crashing fury of a mill race. With modern technology achieving water movement is simple, for we now have a wide range of easily installed submersible pumps and a multitude of accessories. Whether it is a simple waterfall or fountain that you desire, or a feature with lights that flash in time to music synchronized with dancing jets of water, the options are all there. What is more, most are readily available at your local garden center.

While moving water adds much to the garden, especially sounds and contrasting light patterns, it does not come without cost, for many of the most popular aquatic plants that we enjoy dislike moving water. Thus, careful thought must be given to the arrangement of water flow so that plants can be introduced without problems.

The aquatic plants used in water gardening belong to two distinct groups: those that are naturally inhabitants of pools and quiet backwaters, and others that grow at the streamside and that tolerate rushing water and its rise and fall. The former include water lilies and deepwater aquatics such as water hawthorn (*Aponogeton distachyos*), and water fringe (*Nymphoides peltata*), while the latter embrace most of the marginal plants such as irises and bulrushes. Floating plants are hopeless in a feature with moving water as they get pushed into a heap at one end of the pool. Submerged plants take it all in their stride, however. Whatever the moving water feature you desire, however turbulent the water, there are some plants that will grow perfectly contentedly in such a situation. It is just that moving water limits choice.

In many cases the water feature itself is the object of attention and plants play no part in the visual scheme. Indeed, at the other end of the scale, it could be said that some of the more elaborate fountains are really liquid sculptures, such is the technology and power available to manipulate water. Add to this the effects that can be created by introducing colored light and the prospects for innovation are clear.

Of course all the myriad commercial products associated with moving water are only a means to an end. With a little imagination and the use of commonly available domestic materials, it is possible to produce some really imaginative projects. On the other hand, many gardeners prefer to emulate nature. The neatness and reliability of the modern pump, used with the latest pool liners and pre-formed cascades, means that it is quite possible to install a natural-looking water feature that looks as if it has been in position since time immemorial.

Above: This extraordinary and very beautiful fountain was created by Simon Percival for the Chelsea Flower Show (U.K.). Note how the reflections enhance the symmetry of the creation.
Right: The countryside is introduced to the garden by this flowing stream with its tasteful planting.

natural waterfalls

There are few features in the garden more attractive than a natural waterfall, a gentle meander over water-worn stone into a pool alive with the bright colors of goldfish and framed by groups of reeds and rushes. Not only does this bring movement to the garden, but it also introduces magical sound and the opportunity to be really creative.

A natural waterfall is probably the most pleasing of all the waterfall and cascade systems available to the home gardener, but to get such a feature to appear as if plucked from nature and incorporated seamlessly into the garden requires skill and forethought. The topography of the

Below: A wonderful natural-looking waterfall created with local stone that is layered as if it has evolved over time.

garden is a major contributor to its success, for if there is a natural slope that forms part of the garden scene, incorporation of a waterfall into the landscape becomes quite natural. Where earthmoving has to be undertaken to create a suitable landfall, then considerable skill is required in sculpting the soil.

The choice of rocks is important, for to look natural they need to be of local origin, or else in keeping with the theme of the garden. The quality of stone must also be considered as some flake and shale during severe winter weather when constantly exposed to water. It is important that any stone used is from a reliable supplier who can attest to the fact that it is free from any conservation constraints. Today there are a number of excellent artificial stones that are extremely difficult to distinguish from the real thing.

Plants are very important in dressing a natural waterfall. The choice is restricted a little as some species and varieties do not enjoy constant movement, but there are sufficient colorful and pleasing kinds both to soften the edges of the waterfall and to add a touch of spring and summer color.

Left: This traditional garden waterfall uses all elements to great advantage. It reflects the informality of the garden, and while obviously an artificial construction, the arrangement is very pleasing. Generous opportunities are available to enable planting to become established.

formal waterfalls

When constructing a natural waterfall there are all kinds of rules to obey if you want the feature to appear as if contrived by nature. With a formal waterfall imagination can have full run, not only with regard to the arrangement of the falls and curtains of water, but with materials as well. It is possible to use most hard materials ranging from stone, slate, concrete, and glass to metal, tile, and even wood. The opportunities for creative design are limitless.

One of the main considerations when creating a formal waterfall should be light. It is important for any plants that might be incorporated into the overall scheme, but it is fundamental to a pleasing visual outcome with moving water. The most inspired waterfall creation will look mundane unless the play of light is fully exploited.

Formal waterfalls that are of a preformed construction are the easiest to install and operate successfully. There is a uniformity that makes it simple from the outset to calculate water requirements and often much of the mental endeavor is already done for you so that installation is much like building from a kit. The more imaginative formal arrangements demand deeper thought.

Indeed, with a unique formal waterfall, even when of very simple construction, thinking time is equally as important as construction time, for getting things wrong once the project is well underway can prove a nightmare. Serious problems usually occur only when ambition overtakes realism. Providing that careful calculations are made regarding the spread of water and the flow required to create the desired curtain or fall, then the materials from which the feature is made are of secondary importance.

Left: *To create an even curtain of water, the lip of the cascade must be absolutely level and very smooth. Irregularities in the stone will create turbulence. Marginal aquatics provide an attractive dressing for the pool, but do not enjoy growing in the direct flow of the water.*

Above: *A startling cascade appearing from among a leafy plant at the end of a rill. A perfect curtain of water can be achieved only by using a sufficiently powerful pump to move a large volume of water.*

Opposite page: *A charming set of formal waterfalls that are accompanied by harmonious but informal plantings. It is important with such a feature to calculate drops and flow rates very carefully. A powerful pump will be required to produce the necessary lift.*

canals and rills

Canals and rills are a very artificial, but nonetheless attractive, means of moving water around the garden. They are quite intentionally formal, creating straight lines and angles rather than gracious curves or arcs.

A rill is generally regarded as being a very narrow shallow canal. It is a feature that can be used boldly to enhance and define the physical structure of a garden layout, or subtly to move water around. The gentle musical note created by the flow of the water, which moves like quicksilver in and around the plants, is often the only evidence of its presence.

Canals are different structures. In some cases they can be formally constructed ditches, moving large quantities of water from place to place, often with the intention of servicing a waterfall or waterwheel. Occasionally they are adaptations created from natural water flows across a property. Where a stream flows naturally through a garden and the overall design is one of formality, then this can often be very successfully converted into a canal. Take care if making such an alteration not to interfere with the flow rate, as it might have an adverse effect upon neighboring properties both upstream and downstream.

More often than not, canals are created in order to divide or subdivide the garden in a formal way. They are often used to great effect where different levels are desired. Few plants enjoy life in a canal, and few settings

Left: The formal use of water in small square ponds interconnected by rills divides the garden into convenient sections that can accommodate various plantings. The sound and movement of the flowing water and the use of fountain jets bring a hard landscape to life.

Right: This canal is wide enough to produce excellent reflections and yet at the same time is flowing quickly and producing a beautiful curtain of water. A high standard of maintenance is necessary in order to achieve this beautiful garden spectacle.

would be enhanced by attempted plantings. A canal is essentially an unadorned, formal means for moving water. However, it can be constructed or dressed using a wide diversity of materials including colored tiles, slate, or mosaic. The materials from which it is constructed should be the focus of attention visually, rather than any attempt at accompanying planting.

Above: *A rill need not be substantial to be effective. This attractive stone-faced channel in dappled shade creates all kinds of highlights as the shallow water ripples across its stony bottom. The paving defines the edge and provides ready access for anyone wanting to walk near the water.*

cascades and staircases

Moving water, for those who love to grow a rich diversity of aquatic plants, generally means a quiet meandering stream, a trickling waterfall, or tinkling fountain spray. Such water movement is compatible with a happy and ecologically balanced environment and the peace and tranquillity that those who crave the informal and natural in the garden desire.

However, moving water does not always have to be used in a natural way in the garden. Indeed, with imagination it can become a living spectacle itself, devoid of all things living, but nevertheless bringing a garden to life. Rushing and cascading water is frenetic and exciting, and although mostly associated with the great water staircases and cascades of the eighteenth- and nineteenth-century gardens of Europe, it can be recreated in a more modest but equally exciting way in the small garden.

Cascades and water staircases do not have to come from or go to anywhere in particular. They need not be a major flowing spectacle of aquatic art. It is the rushing and falling of water itself in a white foamy rush or as a dense transparent curtain that is the key attraction of such a feature.

By using a pump with an outlet that pushes air into the current of water, an effect of white water can be created in a very confined space. Modern submersible pumps are quite small and large volumes of water can be moved quickly by apparently modest equipment. So creating a turbulent flow or extensive curtain of water has few of the complexities faced by our ancestors when special piping had to be installed and pump chambers were an irksome necessity.

Right: *A lovely cascade that recreates a mountain stream flowing through a lush flower-bedecked alpine meadow.*

Above: *Flowing water softens the harshness of the large boulders in this striking landscape. When water is associated with rocks, it is important to use those that will not flake with winter frost.*

Left: *A modern moving water feature that is completely artificial. It uses modern materials such as brick and mirrors and to spectacular effect. But it is not for the fainthearted!*

streams and brooks

A stream or brook is the most natural form of flowing water. Gardeners who have a natural feature such as this that just requires dressing with plants or perhaps a slight adjustment of the flow are very lucky, especially if water flow is consistent for 12 months of the year.

This is the idyllic garden stream or brook, a lovely feature fed by a spring and that is not influenced or altered by rainfall. The other natural kind of stream depends on

rainfall or snowmelt and it may not always flow evenly. It can be subject to flooding as well as summer drought. This is a problematic scenario that is very difficult to incorporate successfully into a manicured garden.

The best stream or brook is one that does not depend on the vagaries of nature and that is constructed by the gardener to fulfill the role that it needs to in the designated position in the garden. With careful calculations and construction, a most convincing stream can be created that will have constant clear water and not be adversely affected by natural phenomena.

Below: An enchanting stream where water ripples over a gravelly bed and the flow is diverted by well-placed stones.

Left: Although this artificial stream bisects the garden, access across a discreet bridge enables it to be enjoyed from all sides.

Below: The best garden streams are usually created on a natural slope.

A stream in the garden need not go to or come from anywhere in particular. It can emerge from a pile of rocks and disappear the same way, although it is more visually appealing if a stream is linked to a pond. This can either be situated above or below the stream feature – it really doesn't matter. With the modern materials available, from flexible pool liners to preformed plastic stream units, artificial stream construction is among the easiest and most rewarding means of introducing moving water to a garden.

waterside features

Moving water does not always have to emanate as a flow from the pond or appear deliberately in the form of a stream or waterfall. With a modern submersible pump it is quite possible to pipe it from the watery depths to a pondside feature, which then returns it to the pool. There are, of course, all sorts of seated classical ornaments that sit either in or beside the pond and from which water rushes and cascades. However, for the modern garden there are other interesting options available from chutes and gullies to elaborate cast metal or fiberglass foliage and shells that can be beautifully incorporated into the garden scene.

While the majority of manufactured waterside moving water features demonstrate natural or classical ancestry, some of the most interesting can be abstract formal constructions with chutes and spouts that can stand alone in an uncluttered pondside landscape, or emerge towering from among waterside vegetation like a fishing heron. The contrast of artificial materials and the foliage of the plants gives a pleasing sculptural effect.

Of course, waterside features need not be self-contained. They can be a part of some other feature or structure; for instance, a building will sometimes incorporate some means of dispensing water either decoratively or functionally. The opportunities for bringing moving water back to the pond in a visually attractive manner and yet arranging its motion as part of the overall pond pump system are legion. Modern pumps are so compact and powerful that features that encourage water to rush or spout from the pondside are now very easy to contrive and install.

Below: *A nymph or fairy at the poolside lends a storybook feel to the pool and its surrounding planting. The movement of water will bring an air of liveliness and magic to this special corner of the garden.*

Right: *A quick-firing intermittent jet creates a strong and ever-changing visual element to this water garden. A curious but very effective combination of traditional wildflowers and modern aquatic technology has been employed to make this impressive feature.*

ornamental fountains

Fountains are essentially jets of water in different configurations that are powered into the air and flow back to the pond as sparkling droplets. Such simplicity is not always appreciated, however, and more elaborate means of dispensing the water is sought, often through the use of statuary.

In traditional gardens of European style statuary has made an important contribution to both design and ambience. In its original form it was often constructed on a grand scale, especially where major water features were concerned, all types of chariots and horses being apparently driven through a torrent of turbulent water. Such grandeur was to be seen only in the great gardens and squares of European cities, but these masterpieces set the pattern and provided the technical knowledge for a generation of impressively realistic and very functional classical ornamental fountains to be produced.

These varied from the water carrier and nymph to the comical frogs of the Peterhof in Russia and the small boy or *manneken pis*, a landmark in Brussels. Miniature water carriers, nymphs, and comical frogs (as well as the Belgian boy) can all be purchased in excellent reproduction and merely need connecting to a submersible pump to become functional fountains. However, there are many other designs based upon characters in legend or birds and animals that are widely available from garden centers.

Left: This very modern water garden uses everything to brilliant and controversial excess. A larger-than-life water lily produces pleasing water movement in a pond devoid of plants. Such uses of living plants or animals as designs upon which to base fountains and water features have a long tradition.

Right: The combinations of light and water movement and their importance when planning a moving water feature can be appreciated by looking at this beautifully sculptured fountain ornament. Of a traditional, classical design, it provides an important focal point in this symmetrical walled garden.

Some are made from stone, others concrete or reconstituted stone, while a few are of a hard plastic construction. These sometimes have to be partly filled with sand to give them stability.

Today there is such a rich diversity of ornamental fountain pieces available that you can opt for the simplicity of a solitary water carrier or the rushing, frothing fury of a Trevi-style fountain, or even aspire to a mixture of both.

Above: *The use of common materials in an unusual way can heighten the effect of moving water. Here the cunning deployment of a mirror greatly enhances the impression of water flowing over its surfaces.*

fountain spray effects

Fountain sprays provide a wonderful opportunity for creating magical effects in the garden. They are available in a wide range of configurations and can be adjusted for height and character at the twist of a control. There are fountain sprays that change character in a sequence, which play in coordination with underwater lighting, and, if you want real sophistication, it is possible to have fountain jets that dance in time with music.

For most gardeners the simplicity of a single jet, perhaps divided into two or three or squeezed into a bell-like configuration, is all that is required. This provides all the benefits of sound, movement, and shimmering light that come with a fountain, but causes a minimum of disturbance to the pond beneath where the welfare of plants and fish is of the utmost importance.

Fountain sprays are very easily installed and can be readily exchanged, most submersible pumps having several options as simple head fittings that merely push or screw onto the pump outlet. So it is possible to ring the changes from day to day, depending upon your mood or the changing climate. When the weather is hot, a substantial outflow is desirable creating splashing and turbulence,

but on a still dull day the gentle tinkling of water from a solitary jet can be most effective.

Another startling effect can be created by the bold physical twisting and cascading of a vigorous spout of water or geyser. These are liquid sculptures that can become an essential part of the garden landscape. Such a sculpture can be switched off to leave a placid surface, but when activated it arises like a water phoenix and creates a special focus that should be treasured.

Above: *Some water features are dominated by moving water. There is no place for plants or water gardening here, for it is the physical effect created by the water that creates the focus of attention. Such a noisy and sparkling spray can be easily created with a relatively powerful submersible pump.*

Above: *A simple but very effective fountain created by a standard jet fitting attached to a basic submersible pump placed in the pool. The height of the spray complements the planting around the pool.*

Left: *A lazy bubbling fountain that brings quiet movement to this peaceful corner. It is easily created by the use of selected fountain jets and accurate control of the water flow.*

wall fountains and grottoes

It is possible to enjoy moving water without a pond, but in a confined space it can be difficult to achieve this effectively. Wall fountains and grottoes provide the imaginative gardener with a viable option, both for home construction and for building in kit form. Indeed, some wall fountains are completely self-contained and merely require hanging on the wall, filling with water, and connecting to an electrical supply.

There are a number of masks and gargoyles that can be used to spout water into a container below. This may be a small pool or just a modest bowl or dish. In some cases the water may not be circulated directly from this, but rather from a reservoir or sump hidden behind or beneath the display. In this way the only visible feature is the gargoyle or wall mask from which a stream of water gently spouts.

Grottoes are wonderful adjuncts to a garden. They conjure up a mystical or contemplative atmosphere and can become important focal points in the garden. Simplicity is the keynote for a grotto's success. Plain moss-covered stones and gentle dripping water conjure up the image of legends, while in the family suburban garden a grotto can become the haunt of friendly garden gnomes and fairies, much to the delight of small children.

Of all the moving water features, wall fountains and grottoes probably offer the greatest freedom of expression for they can be whatever you want them to be—traditional, modern, mystical, or abstract. With these features the unconventional gardener can get away with almost anything!

Above: *An interesting concept is this fountain in reverse. Inside the grotto the water is directed downward from the ceiling into a pool below.*

Right: *The art of moving water in the classical style. This grotto embraces all traditions from clamshells and a mask of Apollo to tufa rock.*

self-contained fountain features

There are many fountain features that are completely self-contained, and a number of them are also portable. Although considered to be the prerogative of the small garden, courtyard, or terrace, there is no reason at all why tub and pot fountains, bubblers, and millstones should not also be part of the greater garden landscape. All the compact bubbling water features that have become so popular in the small domestic garden can equally be used in selected intimate corners in larger gardens.

Above: *Self-contained water features are excellent, for they can be enjoyed alone, or else – as here – integrated fully and effectively into the garden as a focal point of interest.*

The diversity of small fountain features is enormous, for with an electrical supply and a small submersible pump, almost any type of a fountain can be contrived in a watertight container. The most popular are bubblers created in tubs and jars. These comprise a container into which the pump is lowered; a strong metal grill is then placed above the pump, but with sufficient room left to the rim of the container to accommodate a generous layer of cobblestones. The container is filled with water, the outlet pipe concealed among the stones, and the pump switched on. The bubbler produces a very pleasing effect as the water gurgles over the cobblestones and drips back into the container.

Left: *These large stones are impressive in themselves, but with water flowing over them they take on another dimension. Eventually algal deposits will produce a weathered appearance.*

Above: *Instead of elaborate topiary shapes providing the centerpieces of this traditional parterre, small water features have been introduced with elegant dancing fountains.*

The same principles involve the use of moving water in a range of containers, from strawberry and herb pots to old sinks and galvanized tubs. Sometimes containers are buried up to their rims in the ground. In this case, it matters little what the container looks like, especially if it is top-dressed with cobblestones.

Millstones operate on a similar principle, water emerging from the hole in the center and cascading over the surface of the stone to drip through cobblestones into a reservoir buried below. Such a reservoir may be made with a pond liner although it also is possible to buy a millstone with a matching preformed reservoir.

basic design and construction

While it is relatively simple with modern equipment to create a moving water feature of some kind, it is important to ensure that even with completely self-contained features, basic principles are respected. Even where there are no plants involved, positioning of the feature is critical, both practically and aesthetically.

Water features that include plants must have full light in order that the plants prosper, but where water alone is involved, then it is equally desirable that it should be well lit, for there is little more magical in the garden than the glint of sunlight on a falling curtain of water. The position should also be sheltered from the wind, for the fall of a fountain can be disrupted and the effect ruined if located on a breezy corner. Not only is this aesthetically undesirable, but splashing water on path or patio is not pleasing either.

Otherwise, a moving water feature can be placed anywhere desired. Whether attached to a pond or freestanding, there is complete freedom of location.

Above: *When considering the placement of a water feature, it is important to mark out the area, taking into account local features such as the shade cast by trees and incline.*

LAYING AN ELECTRIC CABLE

1 *It is important when laying an electrical cable to a water feature to ensure that it is covered adequately with soil in a deep trench, and that it is manufactured for outdoor use. An armored cable (left) is to be preferred.*

2 *To protect a buried cable from accidental excavation damage, cover it with a layer of sand and lay a row of tiles across the top. The chances of the cable being disturbed by a thrusting spade are remote.*

3 *Once the tiles are securely installed, stick a hazard tape on them. These tapes are weather- and rot-proof and give an early warning of impending danger if digging or other earthmoving activities take place in the immediate vicinity.*

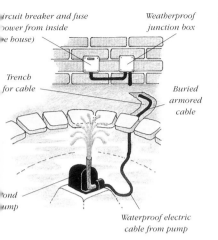

ircuit breaker and fuse
power from inside
he house)

Weatherproof
junction box

Trench
for cable

Buried
armored
cable

'ond
ump

Waterproof electric
cable from pump

Electrical wiring to the pond

Right: A pleasing well-balanced pool with accompanying waterfall. This demonstrates how, despite its limitations, moving water can be incorporated into the garden without causing any problems to fish or planting.

Above: It is important to get the shape of a pool and stream right before the first turf is cut. Mark out the shape on the ground with hose or rope. Check that everything works visually, and also practically with regard to the lie of the land.

However, if constructing a waterfall, it can be both useful and pleasing to the eye to utilize existing landform. Man-made mounds can be carefully sculpted and incorporated into the landscape, but natural topography is generally superior.

Safety should also be a high priority both from the point of view of young children being in close proximity to open water, and also the supply of electricity to power the pump. The provision of proper waterproof connectors for cables and their safe installation beneath the soil are major considerations. There are other considerations that are as important as the purely visual aspects. For example, a waterfall should be set up so that when the pump is switched off water still remains in the cascade basins. If you build your basins with a forward tilt, the water will drain away and you will be faced with an unsightly dry water course. This is typical of the many small considerations that must be made. They indicate the importance of carefully thinking through the design of a moving water feature project before starting construction.

options and materials

The gardener who wishes to create a waterfall or fountain has many options. It is not necessary to put together a complex proposal, for at the garden center all kinds of exciting opportunities await the enthusiast. Preformed waterfalls and cascade units take so much of the work out of creating such a feature. Not only are they guaranteed to be watertight, but they are of such a configuration that when the pump is switched off, some water remains lying in the units.

Pumps are often included as part of a package, and sometimes, as with a wall fountain, are built into the structure. There are very elaborate kits around where it is not necessary to know anything about the pump, other than that it is attached and will function adequately if connected to the electrical supply. This is particularly evident with wooden tubs and traditional village pump arrangements.

There are a whole range of ready-made fountains that comprise an ornament and a pump that just need placing in the pool and switching on. Some are tiny and can be used in pot or container arrangement, while others are gushing jets in the best traditions of classical designs and require a generous spread of water.

Modern interchangeable hoses, connectors, valves, and couplings all provide instant watertight connections that enable the water gardener to put together innovative designs if the package or kit is not appealing. No longer are soldering and brazing essential skills for constructing exciting and unusual creations. A spanner and screwdriver are usually all that is required.

HOSES, CONNECTORS, TAPS, AND COUPLINGS

This page: There is a wide range of pipes and easily installed pipe fittings available off the shelf at the garden center or plumbing supply store. These make the production of quite elaborate arrangements simple, even for the beginner. The most versatile and durable pipe is ridged like a vacuum cleaner hose.

Right: A waterfall can be an absolute joy when illuminated in the evening. Here all the elements of moving water, pool, and plants have come together and are enhanced by carefully placed lights. These are easy to install and not expensive to maintain. They add a new dimension to the garden.

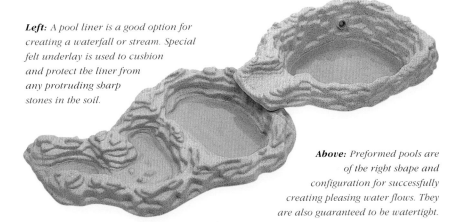

Left: A pool liner is a good option for creating a waterfall or stream. Special felt underlay is used to cushion and protect the liner from any protruding sharp stones in the soil.

Above: Preformed pools are of the right shape and configuration for successfully creating pleasing water flows. They are also guaranteed to be watertight.

pumps and filters

There are two main kinds of pumps: submersible and surface. For most gardeners the surface kinds are now of little relevance for they are employed only to displace very large volumes of water and are rarely necessary in a domestic situation. Apart from their scale, surface pumps demand a specially constructed brick chamber and often very elaborate pipework that is mostly beyond the capabilities of the average handyman.

Above: *This pump does not move water but it distributes air into the water and is intended as a means of oxygenating a pool where there is a large population of fish.*

The component parts of a modern submersible pump showing the power unit, impeller, impeller housing, fountain jet with dual output to both fountainhead and waterfall, filter foam, and the filter strainer.

Submersible pumps are available in wide variety and can fulfill most of the requirements of the average pond owner. Even quite compact units can thrust a significant jet of water into the air and at the same time produce a pleasing waterfall. There are also miniature pumps that can conversely yield a modest flow compatible with the tiniest container feature.

Filters are also useful adjuncts to a pump, especially in a pool where there is no prospect of natural balance, as is usually the case where moving water dominates. There are four main filtration systems each suited to a different role, but the mechanical kind is the one usually associated with fountains. This is a system that physically removes suspended particles and debris by passing water through a filter medium. The others involve chemical or biological action or else UV light.

With a pump the most important factor is the flow rate – the amount of water that the pump displaces per minute or hour and the effect that has upon the feature. A simple test to calculate the necessary capacity involves measuring the desired water flow for one minute, converting it into gallons or liters and multiplying the figure by 60 to give a flow rate per hour.

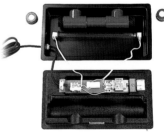

Left: *The ultraviolet filter is effective against all algae. Water that is laden with suspended algae returns to the pond clear. UV filtration is the most reliable method of ensuring clear water where a natural balance is impossible to establish.*

Right: *Before purchasing a pump it is important to ensure that the water flow rate is right. The figure can be established by running a pipe into the cascade unit at a rate that satisfies you and measuring the water flowing over it for the period of a minute.*

TAKING A PUMP APART

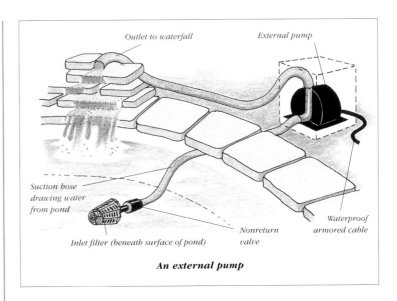

An external pump

Outlet to waterfall

External pump

Suction hose drawing water from pond

Inlet filter (beneath surface of pond)

Nonreturn valve

Waterproof armored cable

An external pump

1 *Submersible pumps are constructed in simple sections that pull apart. In order to get into the pump, it is essential first to remove the shroud that covers the filter foam.*

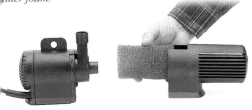

2 *Once the shroud or strainer has been separated, the filter foam is revealed. It is periodically necessary to remove this for cleaning.*

3 *In order to clean the pump thoroughly, it is necessary to remove the impeller that lies behind a casing like this. It is located in the part of the pump with the motor. It is this that moves the water.*

4 *Gently remove the impeller with a firm tug. It contains a powerful magnet and requires a stronger pull than may at first be presumed.*

Left: *This is a multibrush filter unit. The filter brushes take out most of the suspended material. The additional filter medium then works both mechanically and biologically. Colonies of bacteria grow on the medium, and they convert fish waste into harmless nitrates.*

Right: *A compact filter that may be used both in and out of a pool. It operates using a ceramic filter medium. This is placed in the bottom and a thick filter sponge is added. The lid and outlet pipe is then attached. Filters like this help to maintain water clarity.*

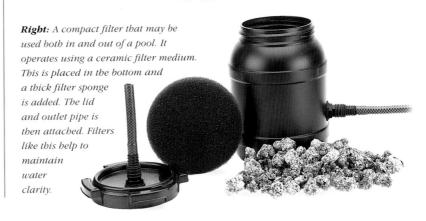

header pools and reservoirs

There is little difference in function between a header pool and a reservoir. The header pool is usually decorative and functional, while the reservoir is purely functional. Header pools are the small shallow pools that serve to feed waterfalls. They are situated above a cascade or waterfall feature and water is directed into them via a hose from the pump. Although it is possible to grow some small aquatic plants in a header pool, it is not usually desirable, either from the point of view of overwintering or interference with maintenance.

Reservoirs are usually hidden from view. They mostly comprise tanks and are often completely enclosed. Solely functional, they offer opportunities for storing considerably larger quantities of water than are available from a header pool. Reservoirs are not necessary at the summit of a waterfall or cascade, but they can provide a very useful service in the ground beneath a fountain or other moving water feature.

Sometimes a submersible pump is accommodated in a reservoir unit. This is particularly useful when the pool part of the water feature is of insufficient depth for the pump to function successfully or if the pump is going to be highly visible. In the case of wall fountains, such a reservoir is recommended, as the collecting pool is often very shallow.

Above: *Streams like this are often fed from a reservoir. Water is pumped from it to a header pool at the top of the water feature.*

Right: *Header pools are important for the successful establishment of moving water. Here a pot is allowed to fill up and overflow so that water cascades down a brick and tile water course. Here the header pool has become an integral part of the feature.*

SINKING A RESERVOIR

1 *Measure your reservoir and transfer the measurement to the ground by scoring the outline of the tank in the grass or soil.*

2 *Cut around the mark created by the stick and line with an edging iron or sharp spade to simplify turf lifting.*

3 *Excavate a hole to the required depth and place the reservoir in it. Backfill around the edges with soil.*

a waterfall from preformed units

There are many and varied preformed waterfall and cascade units that can be added to a pool. Some look very natural, but others are hideous, so take time to select appropriate units carefully and be aware of how much will still be exposed once they are installed.

Some preformed units are single structures, while others comprise a series of separate sections of different configuration that offer imaginative design opportunities. None of the preformed units, whether reconstituted stone, plastic, or fiberglass are easy to install from the visual point of view. They really look convincing only when they are dressed with rocks and heavily planted. However, they are completely watertight and if installed correctly should become a leakproof feature.

Preformed waterfall and cascade units have to be installed on a slope. This may be a natural feature or else created by soil profiling, but should be both tall and wide enough to accommodate their length and breadth without giving a cramped appearance. If an artificial mound has to be created, it should ideally be allowed to settle over the winter period. Installing preformed units on freshly disturbed soil results in slippage and the whole construction process may have to be started again.

Preformed units can also be installed in a more formal way where the land is terraced. They can be included very satisfactorily as an integral part of a formal water arrangement secured between stone or brick walls. The options for their imaginative use are unlimited.

To be really successful, their foundations must be firm and level. Unsettled soil that causes twisting and seepage can be a major problem. With new constructions, create a secure mound of hardcore and cover it with soil.

MAKING A WATERFALL FROM PREFORMED UNITS

1 *To avoid the outlet hose from the pump showing above the water, drill a small hole through the back, ideally below the point at which the water level will rest in the upper part of the unit.*

2 *It is vital to seal the joint with the input hose with a waterproof sealant so that there is no chance of water escaping. Any seepage behind the unit may result in soil slippage.*

3 *Allow the sealant to set properly after introducing the fitting. The outlet pipe is trimmed so that the fitting can be fixed securely with a plastic nut screwed flush to the unit.*

4 *An excavation larger than the cascade units is prepared to permit room for adjustment. The units are then placed in their final positions, bricks being used behind as necessary for packing.*

5 *The soil is then replaced carefully beneath and around the units. It is important that it fills all the voids.*

6 *When everything is finally in place and backfilled, it should be checked with a level. Also test the flow of water to see that it falls as you want it to.*

7 *The finished feature planted with water flowing freely – a simple method of introducing moving water into the garden.*

Above: *Preformed cascade units come in all shapes and sizes. Here an effective design of scalloped bowls lets water tumble down four levels.*

making a waterfall using liner

A pool liner offers the most flexible method of creating a waterfall or cascade. An excavation can be created and lined that reflects exactly the intentions of the designer. Preformed cascade and waterfall units are very inflexible compared with a liner, but they do have the advantage of being watertight if installed correctly. The greatest danger with a liner construction is not so much the risk of puncturing, but seepage around the edges if these are not very carefully finished.

When excavating a liner waterfall, commence work next to the pool and then progress up the incline. As with a mound for preformed units, it is equally important that the soil into which the liner is to be placed is compacted. This can be done artificially, but is much better achieved by full settlement following winter rain. Any sinking after the liner is installed may result in seepage.

With a lined construction there are often facings of rock and a covering of gravel or shingle. These can be arranged to produce wonderful effects, but always remember that it is the solid soil foundation and the protective layer of pool liner that enables attractive natural-looking features to be created and any deficiency will show later.

Using a pool liner and dressing the finished construction with rocks and gravel also enables different flow patterns to be created. A continuous curtain of water results from a smooth uniform edge while violent flows can be arranged by forcing the water through narrow gaps in rocks and stones.

CONSTRUCTING A WATERFALL USING LINER

1 *The soil is removed from a natural slope to create an excavation that is the finished size of the waterfall.*

2 *Line the excavation with underlay. This prevents stones or any other sharp objects from puncturing the liner.*

3 *Liner is spread out over the underlay. Ensure that there is sufficient overlap all around. Mold the liner to the trench.*

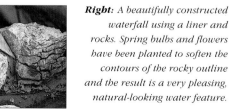

4 *Place the securing rocks firmly on the edge of the waterfall creating as natural an appearance as possible.*

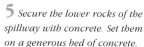

5 *Secure the lower rocks of the spillway with concrete. Set them on a generous bed of concrete.*

6 *At vulnerable points along the spillway point the rocks with mortar to prevent seepage.*

Right: *A beautifully constructed waterfall using a liner and rocks. Spring bulbs and flowers have been planted to soften the contours of the rocky outline and the result is a very pleasing, natural-looking water feature.*

7 *It is essential for a secure, consistent flow of water to cement the spillways at each part of the fall. Try to keep the stones level.*

8 *When all the rocks are securely in place, any surplus pool liner should be cut off neatly. Edges can be disguised with topsoil.*

9 *Well-washed gravel is introduced to the waterfall pools. This disguises wrinkles in the liner and creates a useful wildlife habitat.*

making a canal or rill

A canal or channel is an exciting water garden feature, but one that really fits only into a formal garden design. It can be a feature for its own sake, or equally a means to physically separate parts of the garden. However it is contrived, it must have definite points to flow to and from. If creating a beginning and end point is not practical, then clever planting is necessary to ensure that it looks convincing.

A pond will often be the focal point, but it does not have to stand at the end of the feature as with a waterfall. A canal can equally pass through it, and by clever contrivance can be used to enable subtle level changes to take place with a small rush of water.

A canal has to be very carefully blended into the garden design, especially with regard to the excavated soil. It may be simpler to dig out the canal and to place the soil on the banks, but this creates a very awkward and artificial appearance. A canal is generally better partially excavated and then the soil spread up to the construction, or else constructed at soil level with the water source and any pool level predetermined, the ground being made up to the construction rather than the canal sunk into the ground.

Canals can be constructed of a wide range of materials, but tile and wood are very serviceable and fashionable. Indeed, with the imaginative use of wood, narrow rills and spouts can easily be constructed that carry water in attractively symmetrical aqueducts. Brick is also satisfactory. Concrete is often utilized, but is very functional in appearance and for most small canals should be used only as a last resort.

MAKING A WOOD RILL

1 *Prepare the wood carefully, ensuring a neat, tight fit. Bond the wood edges to the base using a strong adhesive. Clamp the lengths in position until the adhesive has set. Accuracy of construction at this stage is of great importance.*

2 *Once the main wood components have been secured by a waterproof adhesive, they should be screwed together. Drill pilot holes slightly smaller than the screws and then screw them in.*

3 *A small block of wood secures the end of the rill. This should be measured carefully and cut so that it can be successfully glued and then screwed into position to ensure a watertight seal.*

4 *The whole unit can now be painted liberally with a wood preservative. Choose one that will prevent the wood from rotting and that will dry completely so that there is never any pollution hazard to the water.*

5 *A hole is drilled in the end stop board of the rill so that a small hose can be fed in to deliver the water. This outlet can be disguised with plants as the final picture (right) reveals.*

Left: *A rill can take many forms, from a narrow stone gully to an elaborate metal chute like this that, by virtue of its elevation, creates an additional moving water element. It is a clean-cut, modern garden feature.*

making a stream

Making a stream using a pool liner is rather like constructing a waterfall or cascade from similar materials. It is possible to create exactly the effect that you desire, but construction is subject to great attention to detail if the end result is to be leakproof. In this regard it is very important that the area of the garden in which the stream is being constructed is of settled, undisturbed soil. Settlement is the most common cause of water seepage, the liner stretching at the edge and water percolating into the surrounding soil.

From a visual point of view an artificial stream that is intended to look natural is best if created in levels. That is, the floor of the stream should run level for a distance before dropping by means of a small waterfall or perhaps over a large stone to another run. This is much more satisfactory than water rushing down a slope. This form of construction also allows for the pump to be switched off and for water to remain lying in part of the stream, rather than all of it draining to the end with the result that a dry unappealing streambed remains in view.

When constructing a stream with a liner, the edges can be easily disguised with rock, logs, and planting. The streambed can also be covered with cobblestones or gravel to good effect. On occasions the sound and appearance of the flow can be improved by the strategic placement of large cobblestones or selected rocks in the main flow in the streambed.

MAKING A WOODLAND STREAM

1 *Having created an excavation with a firm soil profile, a pool liner is cut and positioned so that it covers the trench. Work from the center to the edges, smoothing out the creases.*

2 *Insert the water input pipe at the head of the stream. Logs can be carefully positioned to define the stream's outline and at the same time to hold the liner firmly in place. Bring the surrounding soil up to the logs.*

Left: *This stream, although artificially created, has a natural appearance. The rustic logs secure the liner as the water rushes over stones of varying size. These disguise the liner and direct the flow of water to the best effect.*

Above: *A wonderful natural-looking stream set off by a rustic wooden bridge that provides an ideal viewing point. The gravel bed and well-placed rocks not only disguise the pool liner, but also provide good habitats for varied wildlife.*

3 *With the liner firmly secured, the streambed can be added. Use well-washed gravel and rake it out carefully so that the liner is completely hidden.*

4 *Larger stones are then incorporated. These disguise the input pipe, and others are positioned strategically in the streambed to direct the water.*

5 *Top-dress the surrounding area with wood chips. The finished level should be below the edge of the logs to avoid runoff after rain.*

making a poolside feature

Moving water usually emanates from within the pond or else rushes over a waterfall or cascade, but it is also perfectly possible to arrange for it to feature at the side of the pond. The submersible pump is placed within the pond and the delivery hose carried to the top of the feature in much the same way as with a waterfall. It is important with such a feature to have a sufficiently powerful pump, for often there is a considerable distance and lift from pump to the water exit.

Poolside features are often formal and take the form of a raised tube or chute, or ornamental fountainheads. In such cases considerable quantities of water are moved and the splash resulting from such water displacement is considerable. This should be considered very carefully from the beginning. Less formal arrangements – particularly units

or features that are manufactured for the purpose and where a gentle flow of water is preferred – are much easier to install.

At present there is a trend for creating leaves in fiberglass with connections and jets that enable them to be arranged rather like an artificial plant with water flowing from leaf to leaf. The giant *Gunnera* or prickly rhubarb is a favorite from which to make impressions, although the leaves of ornamental rheum as well as the umbrella plant also known as *Darmera* are commonly available. On their own, even if arranged in natural array, they look rather stiff and fake, but once fully integrated with live vegetation they can be very pleasing, creating subtle sounds and movement of water.

MAKING A LEAF CASCADE

Left: *Even artificial leaves can look effective. They are a very practical way of bringing rushing water into the garden.*

1 *Drill a hole in the leaf to accommodate the outflow pipe in the base of the Gunnera leaf. Use a holesaw drill fitting.*

2 *Insert a screw fitting and secure the outflow pipe from beneath with a clip. To ensure that it attaches firmly, use a quick-setting bonding agent. It is important that the union between leaf and pipe is secure. Any seepage will reduce the flow rate.*

3 *Secure the outflow pipe to the pump outlet using a jubilee clip. Ensure that only the waterfall outflow is functional and make any adjustments necessary to the control valve.*

Above: *This copper design makes very effective use of artificial plant leaves to create a softly flowing multitiered fountain.*

4 *It is possible to enhance the appearance of the leaf by using a spray paint aerosol. Use sparingly to create a subtle effect.*

5 *Having placed the first leaf, it is essential to test the water flow using a watering can to ensure that it pours out as desired.*

6 *The second leaf is placed in position. Then put the pump in the pond, conceal the pipework with plants, and switch on.*

fountain spray patterns

The variety of spray patterns and shapes that can be achieved by using a modern submersible pump are unlimited. For the beginner a simple spray pattern is probably best to start with, greater elaboration coming with experience. As spray patterns are created by removable attachments fitted to standard submersible pump units, then the cost involved in making changes is very small. Indeed, it is possible to accumulate a collection of fittings that will provide a range of spray patterns that can be changed according to personal whim.

Traditionally there have been rules that relate to successful fountain usage, although these are interpreted according to individual circumstances. In windy gardens it is wise to restrict the height of any jet or spray pattern to half the radius of the pool. Where conditions are calmer in a more sheltered garden, then the jet of water can be equal in height to the diameter of the pond or basin.

Simple single fountain jets are often used as a focal point, but they can also serve to divide a space or interrupt a vista, encouraging the visitor to pause before moving on. Single-jet fountains are also used in asymmetric designs to offset and balance another nearby garden feature. With multiple spray patterned jets, there are no particular guidelines to consider. Just attach the fountain jet and enjoy.

When selecting an appropriate spray arrangement, do not overlook the possibilities of combining it with lighting. Few garden features can compare with moving water that is lit at night.

A simple divided jet that produces large droplets of water. These are best used in positions where light can play on the water.

A bell fountain offers the calmest use of moving water. It is often used in peaceful corners where there are no other distractions.

The standard sprinkle fountain jet for the small pool. It produces a pleasing visual effect and at the same time creates magical sounds.

Right: *Water geysers can be created in the home garden by the use of a strong jet that mixes air and water and is attached to a powerful submersible pump.*

installing a pond fountain

The installation of a fountain in a pond is relatively simple if a modern submersible pump is utilized. Considerable output can be achieved by a small pump that is discrete and easy to hide. Sometimes a pump may be situated conveniently immediately beneath a fountain ornament, rocks, or other decorative feature. This is generally the most satisfactory arrangement, as the water is then delivered for the shortest distance.

It is possible to install a pump that takes water to a remote spray head, but full account must be taken of the distance the water has to travel and the strength of pump necessary both to move the water and to produce the desired spray effect. In such circumstances it is necessary to disguise the pump. This method of concealment should be as simple and uncluttered as possible to permit access and maintenance when necessary. By creating a raised rocky outcrop

beneath which the pump can be hidden, a suitable resting or hiding place is coincidentally made available for the fish.

Whatever arrangement is decided upon, for successful fountain installation it is essential that the pump is both level and accessible. It should be possible regularly and easily to remove and clean the input filter, as debris getting into the water flow and blocking the fountain jet is one of the greatest irritations for the pond owner and a constant detraction from the fountain's beauty. The electrical cable must also be dealt with safely and carefully, wherever possible its exit point from the pool being situated beneath a carefully placed rock or paver at the water's edge.

***Right:** Not one, but two fountains are used to produce this interesting effect. Both will require separate installation and individual pumps but they may occupy the same base.*

ADDING A FOUNTAIN TO A POND

1 *When preparing a base for a fountain, it is important to work out the scale of the construction and to calculate the height at which the pump must be situated to create the desired effect. To protect the pool liner, protective liner underlay should be laid before construction of the base begins.*

2 *A paving slab having been laid and leveled as the foundation, work can begin. Ordinary house bricks are laid using a standard mortar. For a base up to three bricks high, you may lay the bricks directly upon one another. Larger ones require staggered brickwork.*

3 *The top of the base is made from a paving slab. It is very important that this is absolutely level from side to side and end to end in order for the pump to sit evenly and securely.*

4 *The pump should be level on the base. The base can also support a fountain ornament with the pump hidden beneath.*

5 *You can use a hook secured to a stick to lower the pump onto the base if you do not want to wade into the water to do this.*

6 *With the pump installed, it is simply a matter of plugging it into the electricity supply and switching it on. Providing that the jet is positioned just clear of the water surface, the fountain will immediately swing into full and effective action.*

making a wall fountain

When making a wall fountain very careful thought must be given to its operation. Whether a standard purchased unit or an original creation, the most satisfactory arrangement is one that uses a submersible pump. However, placing the pump in a suitable functional position where it is out of view can be difficult, especially when a wall fountain spills into a shallow basin.

Placing the pump in a sump or reservoir outside the pool is the best solution. This must be close to the wall fountain in order to prevent output from being reduced by an excessive lift or length of delivery hose. It must also be accessible for maintenance and can most conveniently be concealed beneath a nearby removable slab, perhaps incorporated into the paving.

The reservoir can be a manufactured container designed specifically for water gardening, although a cheaper and equally effective means of accommodating a pump can be achieved with the use of a large plastic storage box or trash can, or a galvanized water tank of the type illustrated. Regardless what method is used, the water must be deep enough to cover the pump entirely and be connected to the basal pool or collection vessel so that the water drains continuously into the sump from where it is pumped and returned to the fountain. Of course, if a suitable visually pleasing vessel, such as a trough or tank, can be found that will accommodate the pump, then there is no reason why th cannot appear above ground and become part of the feature

Apart from the practical pumping arrangements, consideration must also be given to the wall, especially if the fountain is to be imposed upon it rather than a wall constructed to support it. If constructed of old brick or stone, the constant splashing of water may cause deterioration, in which case the fitting of a protective splashback should be considered.

CONSTRUCTING A WALL FOUNTAIN

Above: *A most effective wall fountain created with a little ingenuity from a discarded farm animal drinker and trough.*

1 Calculate the position of the outflow pipe and drill the necessary hole in the wall.

2 Secure and tighten all the fittings once the pipework is in place using a wrench or adjustable spanner.

3 If you are using copper pipe, such as is illustrated here, and the wall to which it is fitted is likely to experience freezing conditions during winter, it is advisable to protect it with pipe insulation. This will help to prevent a burst pipe.

4 *Attach the upper reservoir to the wall beneath the outlet pipe and then carefully position the lower tank or reservoir below this bowl and flush to the wall to ensure that it catches the water effectively.*

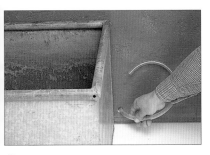

5 *Feed the outflow pipe back through the wall, ideally close to the tank so that it can later be hidden by planting. It is important that it remains easily accessible.*

6 *Attach the outflow pipe to the submersible pump and place it in the tank. Position it so that with careful planting the electrical wire and flexible pipe can be hidden from view.*

Above: *A wide choice of wall fountains is available at garden centers. They are very effective and relatively simple to install. The modern submersible pump and easily plumbed piping systems have made it possible for even the inexperienced handyman to produce a professional result, such as this spouting snake's head.*

making a self-contained pond fountain

Self-contained fountains that are commercially produced often have the pump as an integral part of the structure. Those that are created as individual features using a range of interesting materials will usually have a separate pump, but one located close enough so that the feature more or less comprises a unit.

When creating such a feature, the choice of materials available are many and diverse. Any kind of piping, whether flexible or not, can be converted into a fascinating feature. Stainless steel, lead, and copper pipes all lend themselves to imaginative interpretations, as indeed do rubber and plastic hoses. With a little inventiveness they can be turned into creations that bear little relationship to the normal function of the materials used.

This kind of enterprise is not new; for centuries gardeners at great gardens such as Chatsworth in England and Peterhof in Russia have produced wonderful spouting and spraying creations from artistically worked tubes and

pipes, all self-contained and on some occasions mobile with the pool, moving water creating the means of propulsion.

Bamboo and terra-cotta can also be used to create interesting fountain and moving water features. These include unified and well-designed features that resemble organ pipes in their arrangement. By the careful arrangement and sealing of adjacent "pipes" just beneath surface level, some very interesting water movements can be achieved.

> **Blowtorch – a Word of Warning:** *It is very important when using a blowtorch to be aware of the intensity of heat generated. This is transferred to the metal pipes, so wear protective gloves when using a blowtorch.*

***Right:** The overall effect of this garden is traditionally Spanish, but the copper fountain introduces a modern touch. However, its surprising appearance enhances the visual effect.*

CONSTRUCTING A SELF-CONTAINED POND FOUNTAIN

1 *The copper tubing and fittings used are all inexpensive and readily available from plumbing suppliers and larger do-it-yourself retailers.*

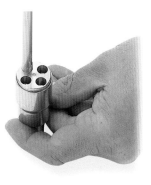

2 *Manifolds such as this provide a perfect solution to creating four evenly placed outlet tubes. Each copper tube fits snugly into an aperture.*

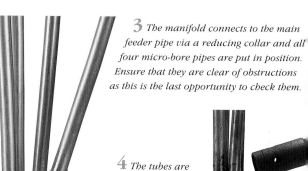

3 *The manifold connects to the main feeder pipe via a reducing collar and all four micro-bore pipes are put in position. Ensure that they are clear of obstructions as this is the last opportunity to check them.*

4 *The tubes are soldered to the manifold using a blowtorch and flux. Although it may appear difficult, creating this joint is relatively simple. This ensures a good, watertight seal.*

Below: *The completed fountain. The pump is at the bottom of the pool beneath the base on which the paving stone sits. Use flexible hose to attach it to the manifold.*

5 *Gently twist the four pipes around each other. The process is similar to braiding rope. Work from the bottom upward to ensure an even arrangement.*

6 *When you have created a central column of sufficient height, gently bend each pipe outward in turn in order to create an even fountainhead.*

7 *Take a small slab or paving stone and drill a hole through it that will accommodate the manifold. Secure this with a strong, waterproof, epoxy glue.*

making a pot fountain

The use of pots as water features is now widespread. They are diverse, decorative, portable, and quite safe when children are around. Some are used for the cultivation of a single specimen aquatic plant, but the most effective incorporate moving water. With tiny modern pumps it is quite possible to introduce a pump into the bottom of an ornamental bowl and to create either a small fountain jet or bubbler effect. The addition of a light to the fountainhead of the pump can create some exciting visual effects after dark.

Most pots are made with drainage holes in the bottom and at first sight this is problematical for the water gardener. In reality it is a bonus, for the greatest nuisance of the modern pump is the electrical cable – essential, but very difficult to disguise. When there is a hole in the pot it can be passed through and beneath and the hole sealed very easily and successfully with a modern silicone sealant.

On occasions a pot fountain may not be completely self-contained. There may be a requirement for a large displacement of water that cannot be achieved successfully by the use of a pump within the pot. In such a case the pot is stood over a reservoir containing the pump, and instead of the electrical cable being passed through the base and sealed, the same procedure is followed for the delivery hose of the pump.

Apart from pots, half barrels and tubs are also widely and very successfully used for the creation of self-contained fountain features. Sometimes these are straightforward fountain jets in a tub of water, on other occasions water bubbling through cobblestones.

Above: *Although pot fountains are usually very much regarded as stand-alone features, they can be used to great effect in the garden landscape by providing an integrated focal point.*

CONSTRUCTING A POT FOUNTAIN

1 *If the pot has a drainage hole, use it to take the electrical cables so that they can exit from the base hidden from view. Seal it to make it watertight.*

2 *Use a small submersible pump and position it in the center of the pot. If the pump needs raising, an upturned plant pot makes an excellent base.*

3 *There are wonderful fountain jet fittings available incorporating a halogen light. This one fits like a telescope onto the outflow of the pump.*

4 *A wire grill is fitted to support the glass chips that are to be used. It is sometimes necessary (as here) to use two grills wired together.*

5 *A neatly cut piece of coarse gauze with a central hole made into it is placed over the fountain fitting and pulled tightly over the grill on the top of the pot. If necessary the gauze can be attached to the wire grill by short lengths of wire or plant stem ties.*

6 *The top is then covered with glass chips and the lampshade added. Take care when adding the glass chips as they are quite sharp. They can be found prepacked in various colors at garden centers.*

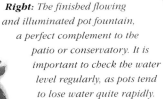

Right: *The finished flowing and illuminated pot fountain, a perfect complement to the patio or conservatory. It is important to check the water level regularly, as pots tend to lose water quite rapidly.*

building a fountain tree

Gardening should be fun, not only involving the cultivation and enjoyment of plants, but also the creation of exciting and innovative garden structures. Many of the stately home gardens of Europe in past centuries built fascinating and often well-engineered creations that produced beautiful effects or sometimes surprises. Spouting trees were made from tubing that blended in with natural vegetation and looked very convincing. They were fashionable, fun features in a number of gardens. The unsuspecting visitor stepped onto a hidden pad in the path that led to the tree and got drenched as a result!

Such tomfoolery is perhaps not so much in fashion now, but the blending of natural objects with water features in various ways can be both pleasing and amusing. Trees and branches of trees have a perfect structure for producing interesting shapes. With natural curves and contortions they are ideal structures on which to build a fountain, and where appropriate they can be trimmed and doctored to suit your garden layout. Hose or tubing attached securely and discreetly to the boughs can create an entertaining natural feature. For the modern contemporary garden, vividly colored hoses can be employed boldly to produce a twenty-first century "in your face" statement.

In addition to using trees, branches, and trunks, the imaginative water gardener should also consider other natural materials for water feature development. From tubular bamboo to hollow rocks, the opportunities for uniting natural materials with man-made products to create innovative water features are countless.

MAKING A FOUNTAIN TREE

1 *The various hose fittings and nozzles that are being used to make the fountain tree are sprayed green with a weatherproof aerosol paint.*

2 *A piece of old, gnarled, but dry branch devoid of loose bark is selected that is to form the framework of the tree, and this is supported with large stones in the reservoir to hold it secure.*

3 *Take a length of flexible green garden hose as the main feeder pipe and attach a two-way connector to permit additional spray lines to be attached. Cut carefully to length.*

4 *Take a further length of hose from the two-way connector and lead it up and over the end of one bough. Attach a hose nozzle to the end of the pipe and wire the fitting to the branch.*

5 Measure out another length of hose to extend up to the second fork in the tree. Cut the hose where you want to split the flow in two directions. Allow for the amount of pipe that has to be inserted in the fitting.

6 Two-way fittings are installed at each junction, ideally matching the angles of the branches to which they are to be attached. It is important to secure the pipe firmly beneath the fitting with wire.

Add cobblestones and ferns to disguise the reservoir. The play of water through the foliage and over the stones is very pleasing to the eye and to the ear.

7 The hoses can be twisted around the branches in any fanciful way desired. The important thing is to ensure that the nozzles that will dispense the water are evenly distributed.

8 When bringing the hosepipe over the branch and before fixing it, make sure that there are no kinks in the pipe or else there will be uneven water flow. Then wire securely in place.

Above: This fountain is powered by a submersible pump located in the reservoir. The nozzles should all be adjusted so that the jets of water fall into the area of the reservoir. Or it could run directly off a garden tap.

9 The tree can either be decorated with artificial foliage if created in the conservatory or else planted with an appropriate hardy climber. Initially the plant will require some support.

plants and fish

Plants are very important for water features, but they can often be a nuisance where there is moving water. Many varieties, particularly water lilies and other deepwater aquatics, do not enjoy moving water and have to be situated well away from its direct effect if they are to prosper. Floating plants are not usually suitable either, for they are pushed across the pool or basin by the currents. Small-leafed varieties such as the fairy moss often end up in a decomposing heap.

Most submerged plants are tolerant of movement in the water, but the more attractive ones that produce pleasing flowers above the surface of the water often get their blossoms swamped before they can be fully enjoyed. Those that remain totally submerged are perfectly happy with moving water, but unless carefully positioned they can sometimes interfere with pump maintenance.

The most useful aquatic plants for water features where there is moving water are the marginals. These are plants such as reeds, rushes, irises, and marsh marigolds, plants that are naturally waterside inhabitants that in most cases are very tolerant of moving water and also variable water levels. Indeed, a number are naturally streamside plants.

While plants are an optional extra as far as the maintenance of a healthy environment are concerned, fish

Left: *It is useful to introduce fish to a water feature, as they control aquatic insect pests. Nishiki koi are favorites as they love moving water, although they can be disruptive with plants.*

RECOMMENDED PLANTS

	Height	Spread	In character/flower
Reeds and Rushes			
Butomus umbellatus	60-90 cm (2-3 ft)	30-45 cm (1-1½ ft)	late summer
Carex pendula	90-120 cm (3-4 ft)	45-60 cm (1½-2 ft)	summer
Juncus effusus 'Spiralis'	30-45 cm (1-1½ ft)	15-25 cm (6-10 in)	summer
Schoenoplectus tabernaemontani 'Zebrinus'	90 cm-120 cm (3-4 ft)	45-60 cm (1½-2 ft)	summer
Typha minima	45 cm (18 in)	15-20 cm (6-8 in)	summer
Irises			
Iris laevigata	60-90 cm (2-3 ft)	30-45 cm (1-1½ ft)	mid-summer
I. laevigata 'Variegata'	60-75 cm (2-2½ ft)	30-40 cm (1-1⅓ ft)	summer
I. pseudacorus	90 cm-120 cm (3-4 ft)	45-60 cm (1½-2 ft)	mid-summer
I. pseudacorus 'Variegata'	60-75 cm (2-2½ ft)	30-40 cm (1-1⅓ ft)	summer
I. versicolor 'Kermesina'	60-75 cm (2-2½ ft)	30-40 cm (1-1⅓ ft)	summer
Marginal Aquatics			
Calla palustris	15-30 cm (6-12 in)	15-30 cm (6-12 in)	summer
Caltha palustris	30-60 cm (1-2 ft)	15-30 cm (6-12 in)	spring
Myosotis scorpioides	20-25 cm (8-10 in)	10-15 cm (4-6 in)	summer
Pontederia cordata	60-90 cm (2-3 ft)	30-45 cm (1-1½ ft)	summer
Veronica beccabunga	15-20 cm (6-8 in)	10 cm (4 in)	summer

	Depth of water	In character/flower
Submerged Plants		
Hottonia palustris	up to 90 cm (3 ft)	summer
Lagarosiphon major	up to 1.5 m (5 ft)	summer
Myriophyllum spicatum	up to 90 cm (3 ft)	summer
Potamogeton crispus	up to 60 cm (2 ft)	summer
Ranunculus aquatilis	up to 60 cm (2 ft)	summer

Left: Marginal aquatics such as the pickerel, Pontederia cordata, *are invaluable for planting in moving water features. Being naturally streamside plants, most tolerate both moving water and a rise and fall in the water level.*

are a different matter. Any open body of water is likely to provide a home for mosquito larvae, and the most successful control of these pests is a goldfish. All popular decorative pond fish are perfectly content in moving water. Golden orfe particularly enjoy the splash of fountain and waterfall and are among the most visible kinds. Generally it is undesirable to introduce fancy fantail goldfish to a moving water feature, although comet-longtail goldfish are quite happy. The use of green tench as bottom feeders is also questionable. Do not overpopulate moving water features with fish.

general maintenance

The maintenance of water features that incorporate moving water differs little from the procedures used for the conventional pond, except that the pump, pipes, and fall units require regular attention. The pump should be inspected periodically and the filter gauze washed and cleaned. Before the pump is put away for the winter, take apart all the removable elements and wash the pump out thoroughly. Dry and store away safely.

The pond or basin that moving water flows into either from a fountain or waterfall must be properly maintained. From the point of view of suspended algae, a well-planted pond, even one with moving water circulating through it, should remain clear. However, it should be borne in mind that because water is circulating freely, evaporation is likely to be greater. Topping up of the pool is therefore more regularly required, which in turn introduces more mineral salts and the prospects for further algal development. The provision of additional submerged plants to compensate for this is therefore desirable.

Under normal placid pool conditions submerged plants are usually planted at the density of approximately nine bunches per 1 sq m (11 sq ft). This ensures water clarity, as the plants utilize the mineral salts in the water upon which the algae thrive, thereby starving them out of existence. The elimination of suspended algae greatly improves the appearance of moving water and also reduces the prospect of the pump and fountain jets becoming clogged by their presence.

Algicides are an alternative, and they are often the only method of control for the filamentous blanket and silkweeds. As they are more advanced plants than the suspended algaes, they are rarely brought under control by the normal ecological balance that ensures water clarity. There are special algicides available that are safe for use with fish, and quite powerful chemical controls for when they are absent. While algicides often have to be used, especially when there are no plants present, they should be utilized sparingly. Water treated with an algicide is not of the same good quality as naturally clear water and sometimes it shows.

TAKING CUTTINGS OF SUBMERGED PLANTS

Left: *Algae become entangled in old submerged plants especially after the winter. While submerged aquatics control suspended algae by competing for nutrients in the water, they often have to coexist with the filamentous types.*

1 *In the spring, remove the tangle of stems and foliage of submerged aquatics such as Lagarosiphon.*

2 *Remove the fresh vigorous young growths. These will grow much more rapidly when separated from the tangle of the previous season. All pieces of stem, even quite short ones, can be used to make fresh cuttings.*

During the fall remove the pump
from the pool for winter storage.
Separate the components and wash
them thoroughly before reassembling
and storing in a dry place. Replace
the pump with a pond heater.

Right: *With the correct balance of plants
and fish, along with regular maintenance,
a beautiful pool can be created that
incorporates tasteful planting and moving
water in perfect harmony. Algal problems
rarely arise with a suitable arrangement of
submerged aquatics and floating foliage.*

3 *Take several sprigs of growth and make
a bunch of them. Fasten the base with a
narrow strip of lead. The lead both secures
the cuttings and weighs them down when the
bunch is planted. Lead is harmless to fish.*

4 *Plant the bunches in an aquatic planting
basket filled with either a good heavy loam
soil or else an aquatic planting compost. Be
sure to bury the lead weights. If these are left
exposed, they may rot through the stems.*

5 *Once planted, top off the soil with gravel
and water it thoroughly to drive out excess
air. Lower it into the water so that the plants
are completely submerged. The basket will
rapidly fill with vigorous foliage.*

maintaining hygiene and winter care

Apart from keeping the water free of algae, water garden maintenance should focus on general hygiene and cleanliness. Detritus and debris should be removed from the pond or water feature. Today, this is relatively simple using an aquatic vacuum cleaner. This sucks up debris and is very efficient if used regularly and no great accumulation of detritus is allowed to build up.

Leaves can also be a problem, not only those that fall into the pond in the fall, but those of associated aquatic plants if all-around hygiene is not up to standard. In the fall it is a wise precaution to net the pool before leaf-fall. Most leaves blow in from surrounding ground rather than falling directly into the water from above, so a temporary low fence around the water feature is most effective. Install this when the leaves first change color. Such a fence precludes interference with aquatic plants. Leaves that fall directly into the water or accumulate in cascade bowls or waterfall units should also be regularly removed.

As winter approaches, tidy up any waterside plants and replace the pump with a pool heater if there are fish. While ornamental pond fish are very hardy, they do run the risk of asphyxiation if the pond freezes over for a period of time. The problem is that the accumulation of organic debris on the floor of the pond or basin produces gases that normally dissipate harmlessly into the atmosphere, but if they become trapped beneath a layer of ice they can cause the fish to suffocate. An alternative to installing a pool heater to keep an area of the pool ice-free is to regularly stand a pan full of boiling water on the ice and permit it to melt through. This creates a hole in the ice through which gases can permeate. Never break the ice, as the shock waves traveling through the water may concuss or kill the fish.

Right: This pond feature embraces all that is wonderful about water gardening. Beautifully created moving water in a natural setting is accompanied by a wonderful range of aquatic and bog plants.

WINTER CARE

It is quite natural for leaves to be found lying on the bottom of a pool. For most of the year, they decompose slowly and the gases resulting from their decomposition escape into the air. When the pool ices over, they become trapped and can asphyxiate the fish.

From fall until early spring it is important to remove leaf debris from anywhere in and around the pool. Often, dead leaves collect in the waterfall once the water has been switched off for the winter. These can easily blow into the pool.

It is important to create a permanent ice-free area to allow the noxious gases produced by the decomposition of organic matter on the pool floor to escape. A pan of hot water placed on the ice and allowed to melt through is a good way of doing this.

index